GERONIMO!

Seven Leaps to the Best Version of YOU!
LEAP TO LIVE

SHAVAUN KERF

KP PUBLISHING COMPANY

ISBN: 978-1-960001-17-7 (Paperback)
ISBN: 978-1-960001-18-4 (eBook)
Library of Congress Control Number: Pending

Editor: KP Publishing Services
Interior Design: Jennifer Houle
Literary Director: Sandra Slayton James

Published by:

KP Publishing Company
Publisher of Fiction, Nonfiction & Children's Books
Valencia, CA 91355
www.kp-pub.com

Printed in the United States of America

DEDICATION

The words on these pages are dedicated to the first boy who captured my heart and enveloped himself in it, Javin, my son. A boy who pushed me to grow up as I was raising him, a boy whose heart is beyond kind, generous, loving, compassionate, and extremely tenacious. Javin, continue to take huge leaps in your life, and never stop living out what God has called just for you! You are the strength, love, kindness, generosity, and amazing creativity re-presenting of GOD to the world. Be the vision you always talk about by taking this Leap. I love you, Javin! Deuteronomy 6:5.

I dedicate this book to my Mama, who sacrificed more time, love, compassion, understanding, patience, and her ability to be at multiple places at one time. Mama, thank you for who you are in my world and the world around you.

Dedicated to all my sisters and brothers who have been a part of my journey; you know who you are. I want to name each and every one of you; however, we would be here for 85 million days. That's why I am saying, "I love you to Life!" Thank you to each and every one of you for breathing life into me when I needed it. When I needed to brush myself off and continue being unstoppable!

Let's LEAP!

FOREWORD

Some call me crazy because one of my bucket list items is skydiving. I know what it means to be crazy, right? Not many people want to jump out of a plane, risking death and losing it all. But on the flip side, from what I hear, there is nothing more exhilarating than that Leap. The freedom you feel as you jump, the wind blowing hard, brisk, and fast, and the view you get while falling, make skydiving, for most people an incredible experience.

Well, you may never skydive, but if you read this book, you will get the same feelings I described above. I've read many books in my lifetime, and none discussed the deep connection between taking a leap and destiny like Geronimo.

In the book, Geronimo, author Shavaun Kerf depicts why we should leap into the seven steps to a healthy life. Each leap shows you who she is while also showing what God can do.

As you read it, you will find a better version of yourself. She explains from personal experience as well as from a biblical perspective what it means to jump. We all jump in life. Some jump at the drop of a hat, some jump when in pain, and some jump during emotional moments. There are others that jump but tend to jump in secret. Some jump when they are alone, and some jump in the dark. No matter who you are, what race you are, or what you believe, you will jump!

The question is, will your jump be into healthy and positive things, or will your jump be into dangerous paths that lead to repeated pain? If you find yourself no longer able to jump, the question is, what's stopping you? What's stopping you from taking that Geronimo leap into emotional and spiritual freedom? Can I tell you that you're not alone?

When I first was called to preach the gospel, I was a tender young lad that had done a lot of bad stuff, and I do mean a lot of bad stuff. I was not a good person. However, in the midst of being a horrible person, God called me. His call on my life was overwhelming. I knew I didn't deserve His grace and mercy. I knew I wasn't worthy to preach the good news of Christ. And I knew He was really going out on a limb for me trusting me with the opportunity to change the lives of others.

With that in mind, I had to make a choice. I had to decide to either say Geronimo or keep living my life without purpose. I chose to take the jump. It was the best thing I ever did! Author Shavaun has done the same thing! I know because I'm her best friend. She's shared so much about her life with me that you all will see as you read the pages of the book. What she kept private for a long time, she now is taking a Geronimo leap by exposing it to the world in hopes that those who read it grow into greatness because you hopped out of the plane.

Let me ask you a question: has something shifted in your life that made you unable to do one of the most amazing things God has allowed us to do, which is to soar? There are several scriptures in the Bible about God wanting His people to take chances and take Geronimo (brave) Leaps. I truly believe that as you journey through this book, Shavaun is going to challenge you to answer those same tough questions. Questions like, what happened, and where does it hurt? When will you get back up and fight? When will you stand at the edge of life's plane, staring at a a future you don't know about, and close your eyes and jump? As you jump, scream GERONIMO!!! If you do this, you'll be able to experience the true gift of life because, trust me, leaping really does matter.

—CHRISTOPHERE L. THOMPSON
ORDAINED PASTOR AND LICENSED
CHRISTIAN COUNSELOR

CONTENTS

INTRODUCTION

JEREMIAH 29:11

"For I know the plans that I have for you, plans to prosper you and not harm you. Plans to give you hope and a future"

Welcome to the beginning of a journey, I had no idea I was taking, an adventure that created an unstoppable spirit in me. Every step carefully planned by the One who created my very being.

I grew up attending a Methodist Church, sporadically attending service, and taking part in some teen camps around ages eleven to fifteen. At that time, I was attending church just to be present and going through the motions, being transparent, I could have cared less.

However, later, a different plan began to unfold. After years of partying on the weekends, being a single teenage Mom, I was exhausted, trying to continue to carry on.

So, at twenty-five, I stumbled into a church very different from the one I grew up in. Praises freely given, Hallelujah's easily shouted out to a God I couldn't touch, As I walked in this beautiful, small church in Sioux Falls, South Dakota, I had no idea how this church and God would completely shift my life.

I was trembling, trying to understand why I was even there. Scared that I didn't belong, I thought to myself, *God couldn't love a sinner like me.* God couldn't love a woman who had turned her back on Him so many times. God couldn't possibly see the beauty in this very broken and dirty vessel.

As I continued to walk into the church, one hand shaking and the other tightly holding my 4-year-old son's hand. He looked up at me with his bright, beautiful ice blue eyes and a breathtaking smile. When I looked down at him with so much love in my heart and eyes, I remembered why I walked into that church. I said to myself, *Shavaun, you know that there is so much more for you; keep going.* So, I continued, knowing that I had to keep proceeding to the church pew.

My son and I continued to our seats, unsure of what to expect; I just knew that there was something better. We begin to participate in these church services, feeling led to let go, I did let go slowly of frustration and fear and began to cry. When I started to cry, I felt tissue in my hand realizing that someone had reached out to me to care for my tears. I thought to myself, "Wow, somebody really does care."

I began to let go, I started to sing praises to God. I then thought this feels so good, I raised my hands a little and began to praise and worship. as the song came to an end, I put my hands down, turned my head, and saw a woman that was a part of my past that hurt me deeply.

A part of my past I was working on healing from. I didn't want to be in the same environment as my past; I wanted to breathe easy, heal from my past, and move forward.

When I was able to, I grabbed my son and my things and quickly left the church as fast as I was able to. So many times, when you move forward, your past will show up to test you, to try you, and to make you face what you never wanted to confront you show up looking in the mirror when you never asked for it.

What God began to show me was that you have to be #unstoppable in your movement forward. Merriam-Webster's Collegiate Dictionary tells me that the definition of unstoppable is: incapable of being stopped. In order to be unstoppable, you have to continue to leap over and over again.

Be unstoppable in such a way that no broken relationship, no abuse (no matter what form), no job loss, no lack of focus, no loss of a child, the loss of a husband or loss of a wife, no loss of parents or those who were close to you, will stop you from getting to your destination: Geronimo Love.

That authentic Selfless-Love that changes your spirit without permission from you. Love that allows you to live a life free from illness and injury.

What I learned is that there will always be an attempt to stop you, from every direction, no matter what you do. there will be ATTEMPTS. Your job in this, is to fight back by getting up; Rise up in pursuit of your purpose. Your fight, is not allowing those attempts to win.

GERONIMO!

So, walk with me and allow me to show these seven powerful leaps of faith into living an unstoppable lifestyle.

By the way, Yes, YES, I did end up going back to that church. You will have to keep reading to find out . . .

Whelp goes the first LEAP

#GERONIMO

"I am jumping in with everything I have, whether I sink or swim,

at least I took that Leap of Faith."

—Anonymous

Chapter 1

EMBRACING HEALTHY

JEREMIAH 33:6

"Nevertheless, I will bring health and healing to it; I will heal my
people and will let them enjoy abundant peace and security."

"Why is Jeremiah talking straight to me? Like GOD, you just really
needed to speak straight to my soul, didn't you?"

An unexpected story from a girl in a small town, creating much movement in the ocean of life. I had to ask myself on a daily basis, what does this mean for me? I would get the answer from God that looked in the form of a movie, telling me, "Embrace your sandpaper because I use sandpaper to polish diamonds." So, as I would softly respond to God, I would say, "So, I would need to embrace and bring close all of my lack and dysfunction?" God softly responded to me, "Yes."

Finding our why is more simplistic than we make it, figuring out why, what, who, when, and where makes up our story. Our life long journey of dysfunction, misunderstanding, abuse, mistreatment, scarcity, and lack of relationships, or healthy relationships

GERONIMO!

You see, my story began with abandonment, continued with sexual abuse, neglect, physical, emotional, verbal, and financial abuse and added sprinkles of low self-esteem and no confidence. My story tried to end itself through suicidal attempts, lack, and scarcity.

Through learning to pause my emotions and thoughts at the same time, I realized God intervened, and I have learned to boldly stop accepting scarcity, lack, and these dysfunctions as my life story.

Oftentimes, I hear people say that they want to be "Healthy," referring to their physical bodies. Although this is great, there is so much more to embracing a healthy lifestyle and living that life out. Healthy: *Freedom from signs of disease, emphasizes the absence of disease, weakness, or malfunctions. Simply stated: free from illness, injury, or disease.*

The very first LEAP we need to take is to LEAP into the understanding of what Healthy is and walking that out.

There are seven leaps of faith to live out a #unstoppable Healthy Life . . . are you ready to Leap?

Let's LEAP! Let's Leap to Live!

#GERONIMO

"Faith is taking the first step when you don't see the whole staircase."

-Martin Luther King, Jr.

Chapter 2

THE LEAP FROM RELIGION TO RELATIONSHIP

MATTHEW 7:7-8 7

"Ask, and it shall be given you; seek, and ye shall find; knock, and it shall be opened unto you: 8 For every one that asketh, receiveth; and he that seeketh, findeth; and to him that knocketh it shall be opened."

My Conversation with God:
"Dear Lord, I am so broken, I feel so unworthy of being alive. This woman that is speaking to you is really looking for the man behind the door that she is knocking on, to desire to know me, and to have a relationship with me. As tears stream down my face, I am desperate to know you and desperate to know who I AM in YOU! I hope that you hear my heart God, I am so desperate to know you!"

GERONIMO!

My journey from religion to a relationship has been up, down, left, and right. Although this is true, it's been a POWERFUL journey, following the word of God and the guidance of the Holy Spirit. This has only come from a powerful relationship journeying of deep valleys, high mountain tops where God always stood beside me.

Spiritual Health is the definition of a personal matter involving values and beliefs that provide a purpose in our lives; while different individuals may have different views of what spiritualism is, generally, it's considered to be the search for meaning and purpose in human existence. Whatever level you participate or practice or even seek out Spiritual Health this is a journey, A journey to find oneself, through the eyes of the Master Creator, the Master Artist.

You see, there are heart checks that we should always consider to be doing and asking ourselves about. One being: What really are your values and morals? What is it about you as a man or a woman that you seek to find a deeper relationship through Spiritual Health?

Many times in life, we find ourselves investing time into reinventing ourselves over and over again. In this journey of finding ourselves, it's one of the hardest journeys that you can take, yet it is so worth it.

You will experience heartbreak, roadblocks, high mountain tops, really low valleys, gravel roads, potholes, flooded roads, washed-out streets, rain, sleets, avalanches, and other disasters that are unexpected. It's the relationship that you have that impact when and how you grow, so who do you have a relationship with?

Traveling the journey of finding out who you are as a person, understanding this relationship, and your purpose in the world is not an easy one, yet it's all worth it in the end.

So let's start here . . .

Have you asked yourself: Who am I? Am I willing to dig into that? Understanding that spiritual health is to enjoy the vigor of Body, Mind, and Spirit, you are releasing those things that no longer serve you. No matter what your story or life experiences are, you must understand that your Spiritual Health is your Foundation. This specific relationship is as important to your health as your ab muscles are to your physical health. The cement and strength of your overall house, the one relationship in your life that holds up all the pillars, walls, staircase, and the ability to have your water flow easily.

As a young girl, I attended a Methodist church. The specific environment didn't speak to my spirit to the point where it provoked a strong relationship. I was bored and would fall asleep in church almost every Sunday. My heart wasn't pulled by the words from the pastor's mouth, and I didn't understand worship. I always thought that it was boring. Real talk. I was always ready to take a little nap.

Although every word above is very true, I had no idea that seeds, the size of a mustard seed were being planted under deep soil. So, at the appointed time, the fruit of these seeds would reap the harvest.

While in Church as a young girl, I fell asleep all the time, lip syncing all the songs, had a raggedy attitude, and could careless. It's as if I was tirelessly trying to complete a Mission Impossible. It's as if I went to war within myself, God, and the environment with no weapons at all. A war I had already lost before I walked into the house of God.

7

GERONIMO!

MISSION IMPOSSIBLE: TO GET SHAVAUN TO BUILD A RELATIONSHIP WITH GOD

ATTEMPTS: 85,000

STATUS: FAILED

So, even though our relationship with God is tested, time and time again, we must, at all costs, strive to strengthen this relationship first.

For so long, I was spiritually unhealthy. I felt as if I always lacked something. OMG! That's a #BOL or a Breakthrough out loud. I was always looking for something in all the wrong places and never knew how to sit still. I have always felt lack and a void.

So, at the age of 26, after struggling with voids in my life and using alcohol and smoking weed as an outlet, I realized how exhausted I was, I realized that self-medicating was not the answer. When the high went away, or I woke up from drinking, I felt horrible, and my issues and challenges never went away until I had to face Shavaun and this realm of my life. Reminding myself that spiritual health is enjoying the vigor of body, mind, and spirit, I began taking action.

However, these steps were not easy. Every step provided some unknown pain that I had no idea existed.

My first step in this movement and the spiritual transformation was:

Step 1. Acknowledging that I couldn't do this on my own.
I remember I had to go through many changes. At nineteen, I became a Mommy, one of the greatest gifts God ever blessed me with. It was a

transformation that I had to continually go through on a daily basis. I didn't know how to be a Mommy or even understood my own identity. It took me so much to grasp the understanding that I had to find my own identity in this process. I have experienced many life-changing situations; this next one, though, gave me the revelation that I needed.

One weekend, I was out with my girlfriends, having an amazing time in Minneapolis at a house party. I had consumed so much alcohol that I blacked out. The last thing I remember was sitting down on my girlfriends' stairs and asking when we were going to the club.

My girlfriends responded by saying, "Oh Yeah, Shavaun, we are going to the club." But little did I know that they were going to make sure that I got in a bed and that I had to sleep this off. I woke up the next morning, so hungover and feeling so horrible, headache, dry heaving, and so extremely hungry.

After I sobered up and went back home, I realized that I wanted a huge change in my life. I realized that I felt empty, very empty. I was looking for so much more; it was like eating and never being full. I began to realize that I desired so much more of this life. Yet, I hadn't had a breakthrough at this point.

So, that following , New Year's Eve of 2006, I got drunk and high and got in arguments with some of my closest girlfriends. I woke up on New Year's Day crying out to God from my heart that I needed a new life and to please help. I remember being so mad at myself and God. I asked God if He really knew me. If he did, to please help me find my way. I said to God, "I will put down everything that I know and pick up ALL of YOU."

GERONIMO!

I talked to God, not really knowing if He heard me, saying Lord, I have a beautiful, spirited son to raise alone, and, at the same time, I needed to find myself. God spoke to my spirit, saying, "Baby, yes, I know, I created you and knew everything about you and your son, Javin."

I sat up in my bed and cried my whole heart out; tears were streaming down my face. I wished there was somebody there to hold me and tell me it's going to be okay. I hoped that somebody who loved me whole-heartily would hold me in those moments before I could speak it.

I cried for hours that day; thank God for my dearest friend living down the hallway. She took my son for the day so that I could invest time with God.

My tears, as they streamed down my face, felt like years of the release of pain, rejection, loneliness, fear, and never being good enough. As I sat up in my bed, feeling so broken, beaten, and unworthy, I felt this soft touch and very comforting voice speak to me and say, "I have come to give you life, and I love you." That same voice that said it knew me and my baby; yep, that was Gods voice.

For so long, I was spiritually unhealthy; it was as if I always lacked something! I was always looking and seeking for something in all the wrong places. It was a never-ending treasure hunt for a treasure chest I thought would be filled with Love, Joy, Peace, Kindness, Patience and so many other healthy pieces to my life.

I had to acknowledge that I couldn't take this treasure hunt on my own; in order to find the treasure on an X marks the spot map, I needed a very well-trained set of eyes.

Step 2: Taking action and seeking the help that you need.

At 26, after I had enough, I went looking for a very well-trained set of eyes to help me go in the right direction. I attended church and decided I am giving my whole heart back to Jesus. I never realized that I was so spiritually unhealthy until I

had to face myself in the worst of circumstances. Reminding myself that spiritual health is enjoying the vigor of body, mind, and spirit, I began taking action.

I went to a church in Sioux Falls, SD where the presiding Bishop and First Lady blessed my entire life for the next three years. of my life. I grew so much spiritually learning so much. It was the taking action piece that helped, led, guided, and picked me up when needed. I realized that my spiritual health was my foundation for the next LEAP in my Life.

My encouragement to you is to invest time into your spiritual growth by ensuring you allow for quiet time, meditation, and devotion so that you can hear from the Master Creator. Each individual person has their own relationship with our Master Creator, so continue to search from within, our way of having meditation, devotional time, reading the bible, empowering and positive books, disconnecting from the world (social media), listening to music, enjoying time with family, just do it. Know that you are worth every moment of beautiful silence and enjoy the presence of God. Continue to do and complete these activities and increase your spiritual health, step by step, and day by day.

Always be real with where you are! Being authentic allows you to heal, transform, and lead with the light you have been given in the world.

GERONIMO!

I had to ask myself, what do I want my foundation to look, feel, smell, and taste like? How strong do I really want this foundation?

So as you begin to self-discover, ask yourself: where is my spiritual foundation? Are there any cracks in it? Do I need to reset the foundation?

You see, asking God, seeking, and knocking on the door when we find it, is one of the tools that we utilize on this journey. Most importantly, what are we saying to ourselves throughout each step? Are we putting cracks in our own foundation?

Geronimo LEAP 1: Pause, reflect, and write your self-discovery on the following questions.

1. What do you say that you are?
2. What do you believe your purpose is?
3. What do you do to meditate or invest time with God?
4. Allow as much time as you need to pause, reflect, and write. When you are complete, say all the answers out loud to yourself.

_____

_____

_____

_____

_____

_____

_____

GERONIMO!

#GERONIMO

"If we take that leap of Faith, Extraordinary things will happen."

—Anonymous

⌐•⌐

Chapter 3

EMBRACING YOUR PHYSICAL FORM
(Physical Health)

ROMANS 12:1

My Conversation with God:

"Dear God, I am not sure I am really happy with this package that you put me in. Yet, if you really love me and adore me, if I am really the apple of your eye, please give me a different package. Okay, I am joking and serious at the same time. I am broken in this body, so many people harass and ridicule me. Daddy, Protect and guide me so that I can feel beautiful about how you created me to be, with my thick thighs, round hips, long hair, and beautiful ice blue eyes.

Lord, what do I say to myself?
Lord, please continue to show me the way . . . Leaping to embrace the body GOD gave me."

GERONIMO!

Spiritual Health is the foundation of every aspect of our life! However, our physical health is our foundation to naturally carrying us through to our life assignment. Physical health has the ability, only if you allow it to affect your mental and emotional health! Our physical health, sometimes, makes and breaks the image we see in the mirror every single day. Our physical health can and will pull us in different directions.

As a young girl, I always struggled with my weight, never thinking I was good enough. I never believed that I was worthy of much, maybe minimal. I remember when I was in the 4th grade, I went to a doctor, and he told me that I should probably slow down on what I was eating. Granted, I was in the 4th grade when they told me this.

I would look at myself in the mirror and ask myself why am I so repulsive and so not cute to look at? Why did I have to be made into such a horrible-looking girl? Then, I would sob quietly, wipe my tears, and just smile as if nothing bothered me.

I had been a big girl my whole life. I was called names and had things thrown at me at times. It was a horrible experience when I was younger. During this time, my Mama, decided to put me on Weight Watchers. At first, I was like, really? Are you really putting me on a weight management plan? Seriously? (Of course, with a whole lot of attitude and resistance).

Mama believed, that she was doing the right thing. However, it did not make me feel good, I felt humiliated and ashamed, and I felt like I was never going to be good enough. I felt like an outcast!

Have you ever had that moment when you are standing in a room, and something very embarrassing happens, you turn, and everyone is pointing their fingers and laughing at you? Well, this was that feeling for me.

So I cried my way through it, yet no one ever saw my tears. I would agree with what Mama said, yet it was killing me on the inside. She had no idea. No one knew that I was slowly dying from the inside out.

I began to find ways to cope with it through emotional eating, doing what made her happy, and doing what made other people happy. I also did everything I could to crack a joke about myself, before anyone ever got a chance. I took the lighter road; I chose to take the fire off myself by cracking jokes about everything. It was when people stopped taking me seriously; it was my defense mechanism.

I never saw a reason to make myself happy at that time. *I know you're probably like, "Dang, she was only in 4th grade.* Over time, I became obsessed with my size, looks, and the sizes I wore, or would fit into. Although this was not Mama's intention and our conversations, it was the perspective I developed and the outcome of these multiple conversations.

As we all think about physical health, what are your perceptions about your body? What are your perceptions about being healthy, and what does that mean to you? How do you see health being a part of your everyday life?

I used to think about health and how it relates to me as a woman, I used to think *"Diet."* also I used to think that I had to be a certain number on the scale and size of clothes. I believed that women who wore any size less than "10" were the only women in the world worthy of love.

Due to this thought pattern, thirty days after starting my diet, I would give up and give in. I didn't believe that the effort I was trying to put in would make a difference. I was always a thick and lovely girl growing up. Many people called me, "hamhock" thighs, thick em's, or whatever they chose to call me for the day. My family called me a pokey puppy, which they thought was cute. But NO! It was not cute at all. It killed me inside every time they said it.

I hit my breaking point at the age of 19. I found out I was going to be a mama. I wasn't sure what to do, how to feel, or how to respond. I know for many moments, after finding out, I was overjoyed. However, in the many days and months following, I experienced much stress, anxiety, being overwhelmed, and unsure how to cope, which caused a huge amount of weight gain during my pregnancy.

I was depressed during my pregnancy, and I was at my highest weight at 286 lbs. When I delivered my beautiful baby boy, I was very close to 300 lbs. I remember looking in the mirror at that time, just thinking to myself that I would always look like this and would just have to deal with it. At that time, I just couldn't take it. I broke all the way down. Eating often, not sleeping, not staying in one place (yes, ya'll, all while I was pregnant.)

I was so unhappy with how I physically looked and felt; real talk, ya'll. I had suicidal thoughts (often). After having my son and being a mom for a while, I realized that life had a purpose, and every day that I got up, I could take one breath at a time and one day at a time.

What really hit me hard was when Javin was five years old, we were at my dearest friend's house, and we were getting ready to watch a movie. As I was talking to my friend, I sat down and looked at her and said, "I feel like I am nothing, and I am looser." My 5-year-old son ran into the room and said, "Mommy, you are not a wooser!!!!" At that point, I broke down crying and realized that my son, Javin, was speaking life into me.

I had to get up and stop believing that mess and begin to believe that I was worthy and beautiful just as I was.

God has the ability to show you who He really is, so keep reading and listening, and you are going to find out who He is in your life.

As we all think about physical health, what are your perceptions about your body and where you are? Good, bad, or indifferent, where did that perspective come from?

We often must pull the Band-Aid off the wound and allow oxygen to breathe life into it; that's where your healing comes from. When oxygen hits an open wound, it may sting; however, it gives breathing room and space to heal. Sorry to tell you, you may have a scar. Remember, scars heal, warrior.

The next step that I took began to transform my life slowly. I woke up after my 5-year-old son loved on me and reminded me of my greatness. I started researching what it meant to be healthy. I was marinating in dysfunction, and chose not to live that way anymore.

I continued to do research all the time; morning, noon, and night. I researched exercises, the science of food, what foods were good and bad, and how in the Lord's name I was going to get there. Your mindset about being a healthy person, must be committed, centered, and focused on being healthy. Remember, healthy living is enjoying vigorous health, body, mind, and soul.

After about one week of research, I came across a fabulous book *You On a Die*t by Dr. Oz. I read this book every day and applied all the information. Dr. Oz's book also provided exercise to get your health journey started. I realized that it was always my mindset that had to change. That shift in my mindset from diet to a healthy lifestyle is exactly what it took to transform my physical health.

I began to eat healthy foods, exercise, and I chose to move every day. As a result, my body began to transform. I did away with MSG, sugars, large amounts of salt, all fried foods, soda, processed foods, cheese, and dairy. At this point, the weight began melting off me (like butta baby, LOL).

Physical health is a powerful piece of who you are and how strong you truly are. As a woman, there are areas and aspects of who I am that only showed up through my physical health. Physical health is a natural manifestation of your internal and spiritual health.

Physical health holds powerful components to your Geronimo moments in life. One of the key components that will prepare you for your Geronimo moments in life is the importance of being aware of what is going on with your own body. The second key component is knowing your family history, and that you have the power to change your part in it. Finally, understanding the benefits of physical health, as well as healthy eating, is what's essential to your healthy lifestyle.

Once I grasped and understood these things, life began to shift. I was up every morning at 5 a.m. to ensure I was working out, eating right, and cooking for myself and my son. Every step I took every day, I began to shed the physical weight once I had started working on myself.

Being physically healthy is so essential to not only living a healthy and prosperous life, yet to be ready for the purpose of your life. If you were designed to be an Olympic track star, you would need consistent conditioning every day to be as prepared as possible for the race ahead of you.

I had made this decision for my health, to show myself that I deserved a healthy lifestyle, and to show this to everyone else. So, a huge part of me knew there was a healthier lifestyle to live.

Once I grasped and understood these things, life began to shift. I was up every morning at 5 a.m. to ensure I was working out, eating right, and cooking for myself and my son. Every step I took every day, I began to shed the physical weight once I started working on myself.

Being physically healthy is essential to not only living a healthy and prosperous life but also being ready for your life's purpose. For example, if you were designed to be an Olympic track star, you would need consistent conditioning every day to be as prepared as possible for the race ahead of you.

I had made this decision for my health, to show myself that I deserved a healthy lifestyle, and to show this to everyone else. So a huge part of me knew there was a healthier lifestyle to live.

As a young girl, I had deep-seated insecurity that was deeply rooted in hurt, pain, rejection, and brokenness. I lived in and through a self-conscious mindset for so many years. Insecurity seemed to overflow in so many capacities. I lived based on somebody else's opinion, every day. The outfits I wore daily, I would only wear them if others approved. I was so stuck in a detrimental cycle that it felt like it just never stopped.

I was so self-conscious, constantly looking for affirmations from everyone around me. But unfortunately, the eyes that I saw myself through were very destructive. Negative self-talk was a daily routine for me; it was as if when I would pause on the negative self-talk and press play on the loving, positive self-talk, here came negative self-talk start running its Captain Hater mouth.

From my eyes to my thighs, I hated everything about myself: how I looked, how I laughed, and even I smiled.

My physical body, over the years, has transformed so much. So I decided at the age of 26. It was time to stop running away from myself, stop hating myself, and start embracing who I am and whose I am!

I had to ask for new eyes (in the spiritual sense), a new way of seeing myself. I needed direction for this journey. So I began a hard, yet victorious journey. Finally, I was on the other side of my wall, saying yes to God and myself.

As the story goes, I made one change; my perspective. The perspective of seeing myself through the eyes of my Creator, my first love. The love only the Father could give. It wasn't what I was seeing; it was how I saw it.

I wanted to be happy, joyful and empowered by my story. So, I told myself that this time, it was time to transform. It was where I got up one day, began to work at eating healthy, and walked 45 minutes a day.

Each day, I would increase the workouts, 45 minutes of walking, and 45 of intense cardio (Turbo Jam). Finally, I made a choice to live a lifestyle that produced fruits of genuine love, joy, peace, and fulfillment.

1st week in, I was down 10 lbs. I was so astonished that I cried and was fueled with a fire of motivation like no other. 2nd week in, the same thing down 10 lbs. Again, I could not stop crying; I knew I could do this at that moment.

Eight months later, 100 lbs. lighter transformed into a completely different woman, taking off a jacket that I never thought I would be able to remove. I did it, yet I still had some pivotal transformations to go through.

Physical transformation will never take place until you stop attempting to change yourself from the outside in. It starts from the inside out.

Geronimo Leap 2: Pause, Reflect, and write your self-discovery to the questions below:

1. Whose eyes are you seeing your physical being through?

2. What type of conversation do you have in your mind about your physical body? Positive or negative, and why?

3. What do you love about your physical body?

4. Do you believe it's important to have a positive self-image? If So, Why?

5. What do you believe your Creator has said about your body?

_____

_____

_____

_____

_____

_____

_____

_____

_____

_____

_____

_____

_____

_____

_____

_____

_____

#GERONIMO

"Love recognizes no barriers. It jumps hurdles, leaps fences,
penetrates walls to arrive at its destination full of hope."
—MAYA ANGELOU

Chapter 4

IN AND OUT OF YOUR FEELINGS
(Emotional Health)

GALATIANS 5:22-23

"But the fruit of the Spirit is Love, joy, peace, patience, kindness, goodness, faithfulness, gentleness, self-control; against such things, there is no law."

My Conversation with God:

"(Knock, Knock) Hey Daddy, it's me, Shavaun, you know . . . your daughter! Ugggg, why do these people make me so mad? Some days, people get on my last stankn nerves, God. I try to stay saved and not cuss them out. Well, Let's be real, I get really irritated and might as well probably cuss them out with all the unnecessary language floating around in my head. Okay, God, I promise that I have your heart; will you please help me understand why I feel the way that I sometimes do, and help me to get an understanding of other people? With so much hate in the world, I really just want to nderstand others. I love you, God. Thanks for listening, Daddy. I will wait for your answer."

GERONIMO!

It's true we have days in our lives that we feel like we have no other option but to absolutely be ratchet, Let's just start with that. So often, my feelings have colorfully taken over my conversations, which could have been more productive.

Now, I understand what I was feeling, why I was feeling those feelings. I became habitual in reacting as if I was always ready to fight. A defensive tone was of voice and spirit.

Google and Webster's dictionary define emotions as the following: a natural intuitive state of mind deriving from one's circumstances, mood, or relationships with others.

2nd Definition 2. Instinctive or intuitive feeling as distinguished from reasoning or knowledge.

Emotions can alter our thought process, or they can teach us how to reach others and ourselves.

Throughout my life, I was told that I was emotionally weak and just a big baby.

Many family members, during holidays, would tell me that I was a big baby and a punk. I wasn't sure how to handle my emotions, so I would hide in a corner and cry. I would cry so hard that I would have a hiccup, crying so hard I couldn't talk or get a word out.

I remember feeling so humiliated that I would crumble from the inside out. Like I was nothing to nobody, for no reason, had no purpose, and have no reason for existing on earth. It was really heart-wrenching to think that because I was trying to share my emotions, I was shut down immediately from talking. It was devastating and crushed my spirit. I struggled daily, I wasn't sure how to deal with it except to stay busy, to have fun, and laugh. Laughter was my scapegoat; it was my way of self-medicating for a long period of time, and still is to this day.

One specific situation that crushed my heart was during Christmas at my grandmother's house. My cousins were making fun of me; I couldn't blurt out, "stop it or shut up." So, I just began to cry. At the time, my grandmother was preparing dinner; therefore, she wasn't paying attention. So, all she ended up seeing was me in the corner crying again, on told me to stop being a big baby, as she always did, or called me a pokey puppy, referring to the fact that I always did things slowly.

What happened next made me want to crawl deeper into a hole and die. Instead of my grandmother consoling me, she reached out and slapped me on my leg, so I stopped, so she would quit making fun of me. If I cried anymore, I would have continued to be chastised for being upset.

I went over to the rocking chair in the corner where no one could see me and cried for a very long time. After some time, my sister came over and asked me if I was okay. I said, "NO!" I began to cry again, then somebody thought it was funny, then took a picture of me crying in the corner.

It was moments like this, in my life, that stripped me of my ability to make healthy emotional decisions. I had little or no experience on how to manage my feelings. For a long time, I did not have control over my emotions. Finally, around the age of seven or eight I started to think that maybe God had left me, and I was not special in His eyes. I used to pray, "Lord, if you love me and see me as your special Jewel, please, show me."

GERONIMO!

Looking back, I see a young girl with a very serious prayer, who was afraid. This young girl became anxious to grow and learn how to embrace herself. She thought that being emotional and weakly presented negatively, believing she wasn't strong enough, wasn't wise enough, wasn't a leader, or had the ability to respond instead of reacting. As a young woman, uncertain how to handle her emotions just never made sense to; she was still trying to figure out abandonment issues. Why did her father abandon her? Was she ever be good enough? A grown woman who was raised with scars, on her left and right arms. Scars that we don't talk about.

Healthy emotions for me were null and void. I wasn't sure when or where to express my feelings. Abandonment was one of the hardest things to deal with. The struggle was real. It was hard to spend time by myself; I always had to be around people until about five years ago.

Not knowing that the Lord was always with me. If I spoke life in this spirit of innocence, I would say, "Love, you are never done." You are forced to be strong, smart, kind, intelligent, funny, creative, and, most importantly, free to Love that God-designed version of yourself.

You see, at these moments of feeling as though I was always along, you always catch a glimpse of light in your darkness. You can identify, acknowledge, and face every shadow that tries to cover every bit of who you are becoming.

When I was about 6-7 years old, I developed a stutter. This stutter lasted until I was about 14 years old. It took a long time to overcome the ability to speak. My inability to speak started with my inability to express my emotions and how I really felt. Many people would tell me that my opinion didn't matter, so I stopped talking and would cry when something was wrong.

Understanding who you are in emotional health will push, coach, and guide you into a phenomenal healthy version of yourself.

Geronimo Leap 3: Pause, Reflect, and write your self-discovery to the questions below:

1. What is my opportunity at this moment for a breakthrough?
2. What is the best way I can handle this?
3. What coping skills do I have right now?
4. What support system do I have right now?
5. What is stopping me from living an emotionally healthy life?

_____

_____

_____

_____

_____

_____

_____

#GERONIMO

"When you're scared to jump, that is exactly when you jump. Otherwise, you'll end up staying in the same place for the rest of your life."

—*Anonymous*

Chapter 5

THINK ON THESE THINGS
(Mental Health)

"As a man thinketh, so is he" Proverbs 23:7, so with that said can we focus on Philippians 4:8, "Finally brethren, whatsoever things are honest, whatsoever things are just, whatsoever things are lovely, whatsoever things are of good report if there be any virtue, and if there be any praise, think on these things."

My Conversation with God:
"Hey, Daddy, I have such negative thoughts at times. I have had long negative conversations with myself and long positive conversations with myself. Yes, these thoughts that I have had are not always great, God. Please, if you see fit to press stop on the negative self-talk and press play on the positive self-talk. God, give me the strength to consistently press play on positive thinking."
God, I get lost in my own thoughts at times. I know that you will help to guide me. That I do trust."

GERONIMO!

They say, "you are what you say you are." So, whatever thoughts you put out there about who you are and what you are, that is exactly who you are.

Growing up, my family seemingly did not talk about their feelings, what they thought, and why they thought the way they thought.

So many times, still even to this day, I have questioned my own thought process. I would ask myself, Shavaun, what and why do you think with such a meager mindset? Yet, I always knew I was designed to live, think, fail, love, and share abundantly.

Our thought process, the way we think, directs and guides our actions. When we think that we aren't enough or that we don't ever have enough, we will never be enough; that's precisely what we will get and receive.

Our mental health also provides visions in our minds that guide our emotions and actions.

It relates to the mind or involves the process of thinking. In addition to that, it pertains to intellectuals or intellectual activity.

When I was growing up at the young age of five, it was my sister, myself, and Mama. Every Friday, we would go to McDonald's and have cheeseburgers, fries, and some good ole' orange soda. Mama would spend a lot of time with us. Many times, we would just eat, play, laugh, and talk.

When I was eight years old, my beautiful baby brother was born prematurely and with acute renal dysfunction, a diagnosed terminal illness. My brother was one of the most gorgeous, yet difficult additions to our family that could happen.

Mama devoted a large amount of her time to my brother, which was a necessity. At that time, he was very ill, spending a lot of time in the NICU (Neonatal Intensive Care Unit). She had to put her heart and soul into caring for him, who really needed her. He was in the NICU for about 65 days.

Mama's focus shifted from our relationship to caring for her son. So due to the lack of time with her and us not having constant conversations, my thoughts began to dry up very quickly.

During this time, I was so hungry to be satisfied that I filled up my time, relationships, eyes, and ears with poisonous, unhealthy thoughts: relationships, music, movies, and many other activities.

The blueprint of my thought process had a preconceived notion about what I should be and who I should be. My blueprint told me that I wasn't good enough, I was only average, and was not beautiful enough. My blueprint told me that I was not worthy enough. That everything was wrong with me. My mental health told me that the broken thoughts would always be searching for completeness, which I would never find. I would seek positive thoughts and never find them.

However, when you build a structure, whether it be a house, store, church, movie theater, or coffee shop, the building goes through a wear and tear process.

This process that may call for you to replace the roof or the shingles.

Yet, you don't have to rebuild if there's a strong foundation, which could be time-consuming, including utilizing finances that you don't want to use on new construction.

GERONIMO!

In addition, if the foundation for the building is cracked, built on sinking sand, and not strong concrete, you have no other option but to start over from the very beginning with a new foundation.

The powerful thing about that is you have to dig deep in the ground before you can construct upward to the Skyscraper you desire to build and maintain. The higher you build a brick building, cement building, or whatever material you choose, the deeper and stronger the foundation needs to be. The thought process that I grew up with was created from a very broken and jaded foundation. You see, my Father wasn't in my life; he walked out on our family when I was very young. He chose to quickly sign over papers for parental rights sharing that he didn't want me because I was a girl and couldn't carry on the family's last name. When I heard that and understood it, it broke my heart to hear that my father didn't want me due to my being a girl. I was so broken, very broken. I had a huge missing piece to the foundation in my blueprint.

This broken piece of my puzzle has made me stumble, trip, fall, and get back up 7x77 in almost all relationships I have had. There is so much power in the relationship you have with your Father. The one that gives you power and strength to be the best version of who you are. When you lack that relationship, you lack knowing the entirety of who you are. Think about this; marinate in this thought.

Funny how you journey on in life, loving, laughing, embracing, enjoying, yet we are circling the same block over and over again.

There are those moments of complete and pregnant pauses when you finally acknowledge that there is a crack in the foundation of your thought process. We have to be willing to recognize the cracks, so we know what tools and prescriptions to put into place.

Your mental health is a powerful level of health to have. To remind you, your thoughts guide your daily life. Your actions (speaking and actions) are followed by where your thoughts—start with what you feed your spirit.

A short time ago, I had a dream; some would call it a nightmare. I have embraced calling it a dream or vision. I was lying in my bed at home, and I opened my eyes to my arms being held down at each side of me. I slowly opened my eyes and turned my head from side to side; I realized that morphine drips or lines were being fed from cellphone to my bloodlines: one to my ears, one to my mouth, and to my skin.

At first, I immediately became full of fear; my heart was beating very fast; I began to sweat and became full of fear. Then GOD gently showed me that this moment was not going to harm me. Instead, it is a spiritual representation of the power of our thoughts and how we have the power to control them.

In a hospital or clinic setting, you typically cannot remove these morphine lines. Our thoughts are in the control of our hands by what lines we allow through our eyes, ears, and mouth. We are the ones overseeing those lines. Once we begin to meditate on those things that we inadvertently feed ourselves, we then ingest, then we act on whatever our thoughts are following.

The well-known saying goes: Your body follows where your mind goes first. Our mental health is so powerful, our thoughts guide our actions, which in turn create the life story that we live out. Have you ever had a negative thought about yourself, your situation, or those around you?

Have you ever noticed that those thoughts give birth to more negative thoughts?

Many times in my life, I woke up late, running out the door. Grabbing things as I am running past them. Running to get my son to school, running to meetings, and traffic is slow. Your children run slow; there are snowstorms, and traffic is backed up for two hours.

It's important for you to find the beauty in all chaos. Many of you are probably thinking, this is wonderful. How do I apply this to my life, and how do I begin and maintain a mentally healthy lifestyle?

First of all, thank you for asking such a powerful question. The first step is, to guard your mind and armor yourself with the entire armor of God every day.

> *"Finally, be strong in the Lord and the power of his might. Put on the full armor of God so that you can take your stand against the devil's schemes."*
>
> —EPHESIANS 6:10

Taking this stand provides a strength that only you can get from GOD and prepares you to speak life to yourself!

How do you speak to yourself? Do you speak defeat and speak from a place of victimization, or are you speaking life, and how strong, wise, beautiful, innovative, and intelligent you are?

What is your focus conversation on yourself? Are you focusing on what you are in the moment, what you learn at the moment, and what is the sandpaper lesson? Where are your thoughts with this?

You see, your true measure of success is dictated by self-reflection. How successful you are in any/all areas are clearly defined by the way you see yourself through your thoughts. I pray that the stories you hear evolve into lessons in your heart, and GOD reveals in your heart what He has just for you! I pray that the thought that you have lined up with the righteous path that has been predestined for you.

Just so you know, there are four powerful tools that can help to transform your thoughts, evolve your thoughts, sustain your thoughts, and grow your thoughts. These four powerful tools are focus, consistency, commitment, and patience.

Take a moment with me to reflect; take this Geronimo Leap with me . . .

Geronimo Leap 4: Pause, Reflect, and write your self-discovery to the questions below.

1. What is your mental health blueprint?
2. What conversation do you have with yourself?
3. Are you speaking victory or defeat?

_____

_____

_____

_____

_____

_____

_____

_____

#GERONIMO

"Life is beautiful; Take that Leap of Faith with me into the unknown."

—UNKNOWN

Chapter 6

YOUR TIE-IN
(Social Health)

"Be completely humble and gentle; be patient,
bearing with one another in Love."

1 PETER 4:8

My Conversation with God:
"So, God, what is a relationship, really? What does a happy, healthy
relationship even look like? Ugg, God, these relationships that I have
are so unauthentic, so forced and lacked depth in it. Lord, please, help me
to know how to have a relationship with you, myself, and those who are
in my life. I feel, at times, that I lack connection to others; how does that
work? Especially since I love people so much, God? Help me to be
vulnerable to you so that I may be vulnerable to others. . . . uggg; I know
you will come through, signed by your Daughter, Shavaun."

GERONIMO!

Your ability to form satisfying relationships relates to your ability to adapt comfortably to different social situations and act appropriately in various settings. Relationships, oh, "dear relationships." It's funny and interesting that although things we are created for; however, a relationship is the number one thing most humans struggle to maintain; relationships with God, yourself, and others.

We, at times in our lives, can really struggle with this. I love to love on people and always have. I have given love in relationships that I am blessed that I did and given past the capacity that I should have.

My deep desire to connect with others created this gift of meeting people anywhere and everywhere.

Relationships with self, church, family, friends, and spouses/ significant others are necessary for our social health and well-being.

When we walk our life paths and feel as if we do not have a support system, our relationship with ourselves begins to suffer as a result, as well as our relationship with God, our Higher Power. Conversely, our relationship with God, whom we trust and have faith in, and lovingly so, allows our relationship with Him to blossom.

As a little young princess (that's what I believed that I was), I always desired to receive the same loving relationships that I would give out. However, there are times on my journey when I have struggled with not receiving the same love that I gave out to others. My relationships with others have been negatively categorized multiple times in life. It had pressed and pushed me to hold on to people in my life when it was time for them to leave.

My sister and I had a loving, laughing, and goofy relationship for a long time. Then at around thirteen or fourteen years old, our relationship began to change, and her disposition began to shift. I wasn't sure how to feel about my relationship with my sister. It just took a wind shift. When you wake up, the type of wind shifts that you know is sunshine outside, birds chirping, wind slightly blowing, and you feel fresh air on your face. Then, all of a sudden, it's snowing and raining, and leaves are falling all at the same time. It's a sudden and significant change in the weather.

Just like the wind shifting, our sister relationship shifted and changed significantly. She began to speak down to me, spoke negative words into my life to body-shame me. She spoke against my looks, my intelligence, and my abilities to be who I was supposed to be in the world.

Those words cut deep, very deep, like a serrated knife. My sister began to reject me to the point where I started to develop vengefulness, frustration. And at this point, bitterness had begun to grow.

As a young lady in junior high school, I truly desired to have a strong, loving relationship with my sister and Mama. I really struggled with the lack of these two relationships in my life. Yet, I loved them both, and God was teaching us all something in the process.

It's interesting when you look back on how our relationships started, how they were in between and, how they ended.

There are very definitive differences in each and every one of our relationships.

GERONIMO!

The type of relationships that we have shape and mold who we become and are designed to be. The relationships with God, ourselves, our children, our spouses, our families, and our friends. Co-workers' and classmates' relationships are the states of being connected to a bond, interconnection. How we connect with ourselves and others is vital. It's the key to opening the door for manifested greatness within you. Doors open, jobs are offered, love is released, children are made, marriages happen, blessings come to pass, healing happens, transformation takes place, and soon you become change agents and leaders in some facet.

Our relationships and strength of our relationships or lack of relationships can make our success or damage it. When we are in good relationships with God, ourselves, and others, we can to think clearly and focus on our to-do list, our mini-goals, to manifest those goals that have been in our belly for a period of time.

So, as we come to a close on touching on lives through living life without illness or injury and selfless action through the relationships we have, let me ask you this question, what type of relationships do you truly have?

What outcome do you desire from these relationships?

May God bless you in your thoughts and answers to this question.

In all the right relationships, you will find that your self-confidence and self-worth is catapulted, your happiness is boosted, and your stress is reduced.

Geronimo Leap 5: Pause, reflect, and write your self-discovery to the following questions:

1. How do you define relationships?
2. Who are the people you have relationships with you consider sacred to you?
3. What do you value in a relationship?

_____

_____

_____

_____

_____

_____

_____

GERONIMO!

_____

_____

_____

_____

_____

_____

_____

_____

_____

_____

_____

#GERONIMO

"She took a leap of Faith and grew wings on the way down."

—Anonymous

Chapter 7

WHEN THE WALLS TALK
(Environmental Health)

My Conversation with God:

"Okay, Shavaun, I know that you feel cluttered at times. I know
that there are many times when you feel like coming home, throwing
your stuff down on the floor, and just lying on the couch seems like the
best option for the day, but doing that causes more clutter.
Shavaun, your best choice is to put everything away in the place God
designed for it to be. God, at times, the environment stresses me out or is it
that I am stressed out internally, and my environment shows that?
Well, God, please give me peace to not worry, the pace of grace, the ability to
appropriately manage my time, and to prioritize . . . because if I don't have
that God, I am going to break down and give up on everything."
"Having, therefore, these promises, dearly beloved, let us cleanse ourselves from
all filthiness of the flesh and spirit, perfecting holiness in the fear of GOD."

GERONIMO!

A letter to Shavaun:

> May you always care for yourself enough so your
> environment is a reflection of who you are and what you
> value—the colors in the room, the furniture in the room,
> and the way it's positioned. You are so very precious, and it's
> evident that you must consistently keep growing by cleaning
> up and moving on.

> So, as you close your eyes and re-open them, look around;
> what do you see?

> What does the environment you live in say about you? Our
> relationship with ourselves can and will be impacted by the
> environment we live in. Those things that externally affect
> us greatly.

As a teenager, about 13, I shared a room with my sister. Now, this room was in the attic; however, it was big enough to have six people live in it, real talk, it was huge, I used to try and envision that my sister and I both had our own mansions. I would envision that we each had our own extraordinary entrance into our houses, lavish bedroom sets, lavish bathrooms, and French doors opening to them all. The colors were bright, the scent in the room smelled and tasted like the fresh ocean, beautiful lavender, and a little bit of fruit. Trust me when I say I have an extraordinary imagination!

I was the sister that had a very creative, extravagant, and sometimes messy imagination. On the other hand, my sister was very OCD; she had a place for all things.

My sister, who is two years older, always had this neatly organized room. Everything from socks to hair and beauty supplies, and makeup was neatly organized and placed exactly where it should be.

Ummm; however, my side of the room, that's another whole book. It was messy and disorganized; I tried to remember where things were, with many failed attempts to find what I was looking for.

On the flip side of that, my things were color-coordinated always, at all times. Messy, but color-coordinated; I know it doesn't make sense.

I would always attempt to see the beauty in my chaos. It was my way of doing it, my way was not perfect by no means, but it was my way.

As I matured and grew up and had my son, I began to have many revelations of the impacts this has had and would begin to have on my life and his.

I had my apartment and started this journey of being unsure how to face my beautiful chaos. I began to experience a season of depression. Not understanding my purpose and going home to a messy house, the garbage that would stink up my house, clothes always piled up, yet a son that always loved, quenched with tears trying to guide me and loved me at the same time. I was filled with sadness and desperation when coming home from a very long day.

I remember cleaning the house with tears streaming down my

face with a desire to live a life filled with overwhelming Love, Joy, and Peace.

I remember so vividly, as my son slept, I fell to my knees, crying my eyes out. I paused for a moment in time, blinked my eyes a couple of times, looked around at my environment, and checked in with where my commitment to God was. Lord, what does this mean for me, and what do I need to do?

At that moment, I desired to change my internal conversation with myself and that I could make internal changes to make external changes in my environment.

Daily, I began to clean my environment as I spoke positive things into myself; my life began to transform. I took slow baby steps, one at a time.

Our environment is a direct reflection of our thoughts, spirits, and hearts.

We don't recognize this until we come home, shoes all over the place; you are tripping over stuff and falling <u>down</u>. Then, when we get up and dust ourselves off or pick up the things we accidentally kicked over, we realize that there has to be a reason our environment is so chaotic, disorganized, and filthy.

After cleaning ourselves up and a quick reflection, we realize that there has to be something deeper going on. Something deeper than just a chaotic room.

In reflecting, we realize that dang, "it's me!" It's me that's dealing with being overwhelmed. So, I am disorganized? Is it me? As you bow your head in disappointment, you realize it's time to reflect!

Look around at your environment, what colors do you have in your living room? Pictures? Furniture, pillows, TV, tablecloths, what it may be. Clutter? No Clutter? Extra clean? OCD?

What does all this mean for us? Here are three tools you can utilize to declutter and exfoliate your environment:

1. Take time to clean our house on a weekly basis: a cluttered entryway or room invites you just to drop all your things right where you are. A clean and organized room or entryway encourages you to put things where they belong.
2. Decorate your house with bright colors: Decorating your house with colors that speak life, yellows, reds, bright blues. Be open to all ideas of decorating your home, yet let it speak to your personality.
3. Organize your home; when you take care of your home, you take care of you.

(Use this space to pause, write and reflect on the things that you can do to declutter your home)

Geronimo Leap 6: Pause, Reflect, and write your self-discovery to the following questions:

1. How has your environment impacted your ability to focus?

2. What have you noticed about your environment?

3. What would you like to change about your environment? How do you plan to make those changes?

_____

_____

_____

_____

_____

_____

_____

#GERONIMO

"By leaving behind your old self and taking a leap of faith into the unknown, you find out what you are truly capable of becoming."

—BONNIE CARNAHAN

Chapter 8

IT'S ALL ABOUT THE BENJAMIN'S, BABY?
(Financial Health)

PROVERBS 21:5

"The plans of the diligent lead surely to plenty, but those of everyone who is hasty, surely to poverty."

ROMANS 13:8

"Owe no one anything except to love one another."

My Conversation with God:

"Dear God, you know that my biggest struggle is understanding finances and the wisdom, responsibilities, and opportunities that come with it. God, wait, are there really opportunities that come with having money? It never seems like it, God, I live life day to day, and I never feel like I have enough food for my son and me especially. God, I will go without, yet this baby you blessed me to raise, he needs nutrition. Will you please show me the way?

GERONIMO!

"Knock, knock," "God answers the door" (With alligator size tears in my eyes)
I am on the verge of being evicted, I have tried everything, talked to every
agency, family member, a friend that I can think of to help me. They said
that I have seven days or my car is going to be repossessed, I have to
take my son to school and nobody is able to help me, Lord? Lord, please, help!
I can't take this crushing pressure, and I feel like I am falling into a
pit and have no rope or help to get out.

God says to me, "Daughter, why didn't you come to me first? I need you to
always trust in me First" It's already all taken care of.

Growing up, I was given a blueprint of money I never asked for. I strongly believed that money was only designed to have enough to live (paycheck to paycheck). Unfortunately, money was not something we had enough of; growing up, Mama always stressed over it, always trying to get more of it. As a result, I never had a good understanding of why I really needed more money.

I was raised by a phenomenal single mother who always did her best to ensure we had all that we needed. We had basic needs, and she always cared for us. We had housing, clothing, and sometimes, needed some extra help with food. However, as I grew up, I always used to think that the minute I got the money I had to spend it, it began to run through my hands like water. I didn't understand savings or really how to do that.

As I got older, I would get money and spend all of it, never having anything left over. From the time I had my first job until just about five years ago, I never thought about the what, how, or why of money.

I also never thought about how positively powerful money was in my life. I didn't understand the opportunities it would provide and have wisdom over. Through my money, what great relationships I would be able to have, the doors that would open, and the powerful and effective impact to bless others I would have.

I have often spent thousands of dollars on other people, leaving myself broke and broken. I would laugh, love it up and spend all my money, not feeling so fabulous after all my money was gone.

There was so much emotional connection to money; I felt insecure, worthless, and never good enough when I didn't have money. I felt as if no one noticed me when I didn't have money.

Okay, so there was this time in college, four of my girlfriends and I went away for a girls' weekend. We got a hotel, went to some of the best restaurants, best clubs, and did a whole lot of shopping. In that whole lot of shopping, I spent $1,100 on clothes and shoes in about three hours.

I had no grasp on the understanding of wisdom with money, budgets, and when to say no. It was so hard. The money I spent was money from my student loan refunds that I really didn't need at all. I didn't know better, so I took it.

I know I have nothing to show for that $1,100, memories, and that's it. I had no return on my investments at all.

GERONIMO!

I know looking back and saying to myself, um excuse me, Ms. Shavaun, boo-boo, why in the Lord's name would you spend $1,100 in three hours and have nothing to show for it? Really?

Laugh at me and say, baby, you got some work to do, you need to seek out some serious financial wisdom to lean on.

I had a blueprint that was written for me, that said to me, my foundation was only just enough. All you need is just enough to get by.

That sometimes, you would have to go without. As I ventured as a single mama, I had to experience life without a healthy blueprint of finances.

There have been many, many years that I have lived in debt, having my checking accounts overdrawn over and over again. I would have deposits continually taken from me due to these accounts being overdrawn. In addition, I was not able to pay my bills or paying them on time was a greater challenge.

I had to learn how to be extremely resourceful with community resources. Due to this, I have been in extremely stressful situations, sometimes, extended grace; sometimes, not.

However, about four years ago, I began to realize that living life through the eyes of scarcity was killing me.

I am not willing to let go and die in this storm. So I began to take a journey of self-discovery and accountability. There were so many questions I asked; why was I spending the way that I was? Why was I consistently living in scarcity, never having enough?

Scarcity to a level I desired to always stay away from.

What was my why? What was my reasoning? Why did I keep spending money the way that I did?

Needing to understand my financial character was necessary. Digging and diving deep into me and the way I was handling money was required.

At that moment, I realized my blueprint was missing vital pieces to my financial relationship. There was a void, and it was an epiphany.

A revelation that my understanding of how to manage the finances I had to give more, budget better, and live in overflow abundance. I realized that I was spending money as quickly as I received it. I would open credit card accounts faster than I knew what to do with them.

I borrowed money from family and friends; to this day, I am still working on paying them off. Yet, these have been critical lessons to have shaped and molded me to become the woman that I am today.

I would go shopping when I had good days, bad days, emotional days, then be beyond frustrated when no money would show up for all the necessities. My financial foundation was so cracked; I was disappointed in myself, frustrated with myself and my decisions, asking myself why I continued to waste money over and over and over again?

It was the best question I could have ever asked myself; it took me on a journey of self-discovery.

As a young Mama, a junior in college, I was attempting to manage my time and money. I was working four jobs, going to school full time (an hour from where I lived), and the guy I was dating had just broken up with me. This relationship was pretty serious, at least to me; however instead of talking to someone, I went shopping.

GERONIMO!

I would go shopping every time that I was mad, upset, frustrated, nervous, overwhelmed, anxious, depressed, and happy. I would shop for every negative emotion that I had, along with some good. Having nice things and looking good in them gave me a sense of empowerment. This instability had grown on me and made me feel like I had power over something.

I was serious about dressing sharp and being on point, especially if I wasn't happy.

It was a severe problem, I was allowing money to run through my fingers slowly but surely and I just couldn't get a handle on it.

It was frustrating, so aggravating, as time went on, I began to experience more life lessons wrapped in sandpaper. I still hadn't figured this thing out, how do I attract, earn, build, and grow income. I was like Lord, please, help me figure this out.

I continued for years making poor financial decisions, which affected my housing, ability to provide, my ability for proper car maintenance, and just basic bills daily.

I knew how to get money. I just didn't understand how to keep it and grow it. How do I pay my bills and then build to have savings, college funds for my child, have an emergency fund, vacation funds, and really enjoy my life?

I was so exhausted with no focus or function from attempting to manage my finances that I just couldn't do it anymore. I was like, "Okay, Lord, I need the wisdom now on how to get, manage, and grow these finances?"

God spoke a word into my spirit of being a good steward of what I have in my hands right now. God shared with me that he would provide the opportunities that I could never even imagine.

God provided opportunity for me to get it right. Although I desired to understand money, through paying my bills, I also desired to live in abundance, not just from paycheck after paycheck.

I continued to dig, with the biggest and nastiest looking shovel, the widest and deepest pit for myself. Then I began to see myself being in a position where I was in line, asking for county assistance. Time and time again, I was asking for emergency help to avoid eviction, my lights getting cut off, food stamps, and for assistance for gas cards, rent, and basic needs.

God will provide these services; however, He wants us to self-discover that we have what we already need with Him and the gifts He gives us to create and grow wealth.

I was so irritated, humiliated, frustrated, shamed, and so mad at myself. Mad, upset, and humiliated because I had completed a bachelor's degree, and I should be, at least, making enough money to take care of my basic needs, yet this wasn't the case. It was so hard to stand in line, knowing that I went to school, couldn't find a job, was so stressed out that I was having stomach pains, not sleeping at night. I felt as If I had to keep hustling and grinding to keep going.

I told myself, "Shavaun, there are great things for you and your baby." I was determined "financially" to provide all the things I wasn't able to have.

GERONIMO!

I was determined to live, love, and function in greatness.

Yet as I continued to climb up out of the pit, life would show back up and try to push me back down that pit. I felt like out of nowhere, a bill you thought you had paid would show up; an ex-boyfriend would show up, provoking old emotions, attempting to pull me back in old cycles that were designed to take me out of this game called life.

For years, it became this heart-wrenching cycle that the devil knew how to use against me.

Until about three years ago, working part-time at a position that was working with young people, my love, and gifting. This position was not able to provide financially, but this was a fulfilling position because it was in my heart to do.

However, I still questioned why can't I provide for my family, keep money in the house, pay rent on time, pay my car note on time, and insurance on time?

Why in the LORD's name were my cell phones getting turned off, why was my son and I not able to financially build or fill the gaps right now? I had anguishing cries to God, like "Lord, please, help, I don't understand, and I am really struggling right now. I need this cycle to stop; I cannot take it anymore. This is too much to bear."

If I may say so myself, I became so dang irritated, frustrated, ready to give up on life; I have had to go to the state for assistance seven-plus times since I have moved to Minnesota. *Look, Babbbyy, all the extra hoops you have to jump through, stresses families out to the point where they just cannot take it anymore.*

Then when families really need assistance, families would instead not ask for help and suffer because the agony of going without is less than the agony of being belittled and patronized and talked down to—made to feel as if you are never going to be anything in the world.

Now, granted, these resources are available to be of assistance to the families who are in need. Unfortunately, however, the process doesn't always go as smoothly as it should be for families in crisis.

I couldn't take no more, going to DWP programs, MFIP? programs, food shelves (2x a month), and donating plasma to live and get by. So, it was when I sat down one day on a broken couch; everything fell in it and the footstool broke that I paused and began to weep for hours.

I cried for hours on top of hours, crying out to GOD, not understanding why my current circumstances were not working out. In those couple of hours that I realized I have been unintentionally functioning out of financial dysfunction. I have been doing some self-development work and was writing down my culture of money growing up, yet it's as if I have been wailing on broken glass—broken pieces of my financial life.

I realized I had been lying to myself for a long period of time about money. I was shopping to make myself feel better, starving myself and my son. That was a hard pill to swallow. A pill that tasted like sour, bitter, shame, inadequacy, less-than horrible parenting, and so many other things.

GERONIMO!

This year, as a much as I have wanted to financially provide for myself and my son, I wasn't. I have had to ask for help with resources, gas, food, cell phone bills, insurance bills, and many other things.

Our Christmas 2017, was one of the most humbling, challenging, frustrating Christmases I have ever had to experience. This woman, right here had zero dollars to her bank account; the bank was asking me to wipe the dust from the check registers.

No money for my son, none for my family, I cried every night for two weeks. I felt so low and less than I had to cry, pray, and keep going. It was devastating to have to continue to experience these things.

So in my tears and prayers, GOD gave me an idea . . . to write letters/poems to your loved ones. So I began to write letters to every person that meant the world to me.

I placed these letters in a canister; each canister was a physical representation of what each person meant to me.

As my knees knocked, teeth chattered, I read each poem, with tears in my eyes, from the depths of my heart to each person given much revelation at that moment that it's not about the finances, yet how you leave people feeling. (Thank you, Maya Angelou.)

While leaving people feeling empowered, loved beyond measure, I wanted and need to leave a legacy. A legacy that lasts past my grandkids' grandkids. So it was Christmas of 2017 that finally transformed my life. I told myself, "I am done not understanding my financial foundation. My financial house has been gutted too many times in life."

I paused, asked myself powerful questions, and realized that I was living and breathing in scarcity. Living and breathing in financial illness/injury.

At this moment of pause, I had to tell myself that I deserve so much better, so does my son.

I am done with us having to pawn things at the Pawnshop, just to eat. After a large amount of prayer, it was as if GOD gave me His glasses to see things through. (Which I was thankful for in many, many ways.) I knew and acknowledged and embraced that money is a beautiful, resourceful tool that allows us to create new, beautiful, and powerful memories.

Just recently, I took steps to take financial classes, working with a financial advisor. Being able to take these classes and work with someone, one on one provides accountability and a level of wisdom that I did not know existed. I have been in awe of the small adjustments that have made such astronomical changes in my life. I am now working on gaining an understanding of my true financial character.

In such a light that, as I built my way out the pit I dug myself into, I have learned many lessons. Here are some of the lessons I have learned:

Know the purpose of money. Understand your financial character. Know that money is a resourceful tool. Budget, Budget, Budget.

You tell your money where to go!

These are lessons I have learned about moving from financial chaos to financial beauty and wealth. Although I am still working towards financial wealth and health, may I pose some reflection time for you?

Geronimo Leap 7: Pause, reflect, and write your self-discovery to the following questions:

1. What does my financial health look like?
2. What is my financial character?
3. What are some of the cracks in my financial blueprint, and why?
4. What is financial health?

_____

_____

_____

_____

_____

_____

_____

_____

#GERONIMO

"Live as though life was created for you."

—MAYA ANGELOU

Chapter 9

GERONIMO!
LEAP TO LIVE

PUTTING THIS ALTOGETHER

Thank you for taking this journey with me, allowing me to share some of my stories and life lessons that pushed and forced me to say "GERONIMO"

A Geronimo Leap always consists of doing something terrifying and out of your comfort zone. I want you to feel that way; change is never comfortable. I want you to breathe in the breath GOD gave you, exhale with a Geronimo and leap into the next best version of YOU. The transition is scary, and most of the time, your knees knock and your teeth chatter. Shoot, sometimes, you even stutter a little! That's okay, stand or sit up straight and leap to that next mountain top.

You can do it; you have the tools already; you have cried long enough, prayed long enough, talked long enough, prepared long enough, and talked yourself out of it long enough. Yet, you're reading this amazing book because you need to read the words across the pages to remind yourself that you're already good enough.

Again, thank you so much for your time with me. I look forward to getting to know you in the future. I am walking with you, praying with you, coaching you, and knowing that I will get to see every version of you!

I love y'all so much; thank you for being authentic with me as you allow me to be authentic with you!

Your Sister in Love,
Shavaun Kay

ACKNOWLEDGMENTS

I would like to acknowledge a God/Father who loves without question, regardless of our decisions. The One that allowed me to walk this journey that I have walked. The One that allowed me to be a mother, a daughter, sister, friend, lover of young people, and a future wife. Through the power of love, restless nights, cheeks streaming with tears, laughter that has filled the room, GOD created an unstoppable woman. A woman that took more Leaps of Faith that she knew she had strength for, yelling "Geronimo in the midst of it all."

The words on these pages are dedicated to the first boy who stole my heart and enveloped himself in it, Javin, my son. A boy who pushed me to grow up as I was raising him, a boy whose heart is beyond kind, generous, loving, and compassionate. Thank you, Javin, for whom you are in my world and the world around you!

I acknowledge all my sisters and brothers who have been a part of my journey; you know who you are! I want to name each and every one of you, however, we would be here for 85 million days. That's why I am saying, "I love you to Life!" Thank you to each and every one of you for breathing life into me when I needed it. When I needed to brush myself off and continue being #unstoppable!

GERONIMO!

I acknowledge that the words on these pages are because the ONE KING that has guided my life and continues to guide my life works all things together for my good! To all my family, friends, coaches, and mentors that have listened to my dreams and visions and even gotten excited with me . . . I acknowledge you, and I love each and every one of you.

To everyone who has been there for me, called me, stopped by, texted me, face time me, checked in on me, help me to be accountable to the woman I said was designed to be . . . Thank you, and I love you! For the praying, holding my hand through hard times, lifting me up and making me laugh when I needed it, letting me know that I was thought of and prayed for . . . again, I say I love you and thank you for whom you are in my life. So, the test now is, are you ready to Leap with me? Let's acknowledge that. . . .

Are you ready to Leap?

Let's jump
. . . . 1 . . .
. . . . 2 . . .
. . . . 3 . . .

#GERONIMO

LEAP TO LIVE

ABOUT THE AUTHOR

SHAVAUN KERF is an exceptional leader in ministry, author, and Image Coach and Consultant. She has spent 19 years in the social work field. During those years, she had a revelation that many leaders, clients, service providers, and those playing big in the world are challenged with identity, confidence, and appearance. So in 2015, she pivoted, taking the modeling industry by storm, owning, supporting, and celebrating the image in which she was created—and, in turn, teaching extraordinary women to own their identity, confidence, and appearance.

Today, Shavaun Kerf is helping leaders lead and know who they are, having confidence in who they are, and showing up by allowing their personal style to express that in the most extraordinary way.

www.ingramcontent.com/pod-product-compliance
Lightning Source LLC
Chambersburg PA
CBHW071019120626
46546CB00003B/1157